Time to Live

Journal Guide

Solé Wright

SUGAR MAPLE
BOOKS, LLC

First edition 2024

ISBN: 979-8-9887676-2-6 (pbk)

Contents

Time To Live

DISCOVER A NEW WAY to LIVE by developing spiritual rhythms that will deepen your faith.

The L.I.V.E. acronym will serve as the format in this day-to-day living.

> L- Lean on Jesus
> I- Invest in Prayer
> V- Value Others
> E- Embrace your Story

You can use this journal guide simultaneously with the *After Some Time* book, in whatever way suits you best. To get the most out of it, I suggest spending a week on each chapter, completing the exercises from both books.

LEAN ON JESUS

The first part of John 15 paints a beautiful picture of Jesus as the vine and us, the branches. The vine feeds the branches and gives it the ability to bear fruit. We must lean on Jesus in such a way that we become grafted to him.

Leaning on Jesus must come first.

Grafting is a process where a cut branch is attached into a cut within the trunk of a tree. The cells of both the branch and the tree respond to each other, acting as a glue to connect and heal where they were wounded. The branch is now sustained by the sap that comes from the roots. It becomes part of the tree and they are one.

It is through his wounds that we are grafted to Jesus. The blood of Jesus is like the cells of the tree giving us life and a permanent and eternal connection in Him. Through this union with Him, we become a new creation.

We are in Him, and He is in us. Apart from Him, we can do nothing (v. 5). He is the vine that feeds us life. We lean on Jesus when we read the Bible for spiritual nourishment, memorize scripture, and go to it in search of life's answers. We lean when we worship in gratitude. We lean when we cry out to him, knowing He hears us. When our strength is failing, we lean on Jesus because He is our strength, our hope, and our redeemer. Jesus is a firm foundation, the only foundation upon which we have to lean on. Proverbs 3:5 makes it clear that we are not to lean on our own understanding. When we do this, our foundation crumbles.

Read John 15:1-8
What insights, convictions, or thoughts come to you?

In Matthew 6:5-13, Jesus lays the groundwork for prayer. If you are in Christ, it is expected that you pray. In these verses, Jesus says, "when you pray," three times, not if you pray (v. 5, 6, 7).

Prayer is like speaking with a loved one. It is the act of drawing near to God so that He may draw near to you (James 4:8). Regular moments of prayer are necessary for connection and spiritual growth. This cannot happen unless we make it a priority and set aside the time to spend in prayer. The Lord's Prayer is the perfect model by which to pray. In this prayer, we acknowledge God as our Father. We praise Him. We surrender our life to Him and seek His help. We confess our sins and ask for forgiveness.

Does your prayer life reflect this model? Mine doesn't always. Most of the time, my prayers are a combination of the Lord's Prayer model and my day-to-day happenings. As you lean on Jesus, your prayer life will grow richer and your connection with him will deepen. If you don't know what to say in prayer, be still and let the Holy Spirit take over to pray for you and those you are praying for (Romans 8:26).

Prayer is never a wasted time; it is our most powerful act.

In *After Some Time*, I shared how my mother's prayer moved a mountain with her mustard seed sized faith. I know that wasn't the first time she prayed for me. She invested her time in prayer on my behalf and it yielded an eternal return. We are to "pray continually" (1 Thessalonians 5:17).

Read Matthew 6:5-15
What insights, convictions, or thoughts come to you?

3

VALUE OTHERS

The second and most important commandment after loving the Lord your God with all your heart, soul and mind is to "love your neighbor as yourself" (Mark 12:31).

One way to love your neighbor is by acknowledging their value as an image bearer of God.

We take care of what we value, and people should be at the top of the list. Valuing others also keeps us from living a self-absorbed life and brings us into community. The more we pour into others, the greater our community—hence our support system grows.

However, we must pour into others in a healthy and orderly manner, being careful not to become enablers or get caught up in a codependent relationship. It should also be done with the right motives and not for the praise and recognition of others.

Over many years of participating in and co-facilitating healing groups, I observed recurring self protective behaviors emerge as people unpacked their stories. Some common patterns included quitting the journey when it got too hard, or retreating from the pain through isolation.

When you are active in a community, or in an accountable relationship with someone, retreating can become difficult. It is these relationships that will keep you above water when you are sinking and rejoice with you on life's celebrations. Valuing others is also key in your own healing journey.

Like investing in prayer, valuing others pays an eternal return. The most simple way to show value towards others is by expressing kindness in all your interactions. When you struggle in valuing others, pray that you may see people through the eyes of Jesus. Jesus commands us to love each other as He has loved us (John 15:12).

People often uncover their purpose when engaging in activities outside of themselves. Throughout this guide, we will focus on valuing others through acts of service. These assignments highlight the needs around us, even the ones we often overlook. My suggestion is to have an assortment of note cards and a book of postage stamps readily available to complete some of the assignments.

Each day comes with a new act of service. Don't become overwhelmed by these suggestions, they're just ideas prompted by the day's message. Give yourself time to complete these acts of services. Consider partnering up with a friend(s) for greater impact.

Read John 15:9-17
What insights, convictions, or thoughts come to you?

EMBRACE YOUR STORY

A great place to begin embracing your story is by reading and answering the questions in the *After Some Time* book, and following this journal guide's recommendation. We will begin each day with the **Digest and Reframe** questions and wrap it up with embracing your story.

To properly *digest*, we must chew through those parts that can be difficult to process. Go back to the *After Some Time* book and review the section for the day. Chew on those parts that stirred you. Ask yourself, "What did this evoke in me?"

Once you have looked at your story, you can move towards *reframing* it. Ask yourself, "What is true in this part of my story?"

We embrace our entire story, encompassing our past and present circumstances. As we do this, we allow God to work in us and transform us into the person He created to be.

Don't judge yourself; you are not your story.

Remember, there are chapters that are yet to be written. God is working things out on your behalf and He will continue until the very end (Philippians 1:6). He is the author of your life. Every day your story is being written—embrace what you can today. Most importantly, we embrace our story by acknowledging our unique design. This includes our God-given gifts and talents. We embrace these qualities in ourselves and live a life that glorifies our Creator.

Read Hebrews 12:1-3
What insights, convictions, or thoughts come to you?

But grow in the grace and knowledge of our Lord and Savior Jesus Christ. To him be the glory both now and to the day of eternity. Amen. (2 Peter 3:18)

1

What's Your Story?

Set the stage for where your story began. Consider the storyline you were born into and how the actions of those in previous generations impacted your life—whether good or bad. Reflect on the patterns of your immediate family and how they shaped your childhood.

DIGEST & REFRAME

Blessed are those who mourn, for they will be comforted. (Matthew 5:4)

Expand on the pause and reflect questions and any additional notes you made along the way.

What emotions did this section trigger and what did it stir inside you?

What is true in your story? What does Scripture say about your situation?

_____

_____

_____

_____

_____

_____

_____

_____

_____

_____

_____

LEAN ON JESUS

But those who suffer he delivers in their suffering; he speaks to them in their affliction. (Job 36:15)

Describe a time when you received news that punched you in the gut. Where did your comfort come from?

_____

_____

_____

_____

_____

_____

_____

_____
_____
_____
_____
_____
_____
_____
_____
_____

INVEST IN PRAYER

Do not be anxious about anything, but in every situation, by prayer
and petition, with thanksgiving, present your requests to God. (Philippians 4:6)

**Pray for the peace of God to guard your heart and mind as you enter this
journey. Journal your prayers.**

_____
_____
_____
_____
_____
_____
_____
_____
_____
_____
_____
_____
_____
_____
_____
_____

_____

_____

_____

_____

_____

_____

VALUE OTHERS

All the believers were one in heart and mind. No one claimed that any of their possessions was their own, but they shared everything they had. (Acts 4:32)

Be on the lookout for someone who is in a season of suffering. What is something you can do for them?

_____

_____

_____

_____

_____

_____

_____

_____

Action Plan

_____

_____

_____

_____

_____

_____

EMBRACE YOUR STORY

You, Lord, took up my case; you redeemed my life. (Lamentations 3:58)

Storytelling is how we make connections. Are there stories you share often that have significant meaning in your life? A marriage, a birth, graduation, career, something funny or embarrassing? If journaling is new for you, write about these experiences first. What is a story you enjoy sharing?

_____

_____

_____

_____

_____

_____

_____

_____

_____

_____

_____

_____

_____

_____

_____

_____

_____

EXTRA NOTES:

_____

_____

_____

_____

_____

DIGEST & REFRAME

The righteous cry out, and the LORD hears them; he delivers them from all their troubles. (Psalm 34:17)

Expand on the pause and reflect questions and any additional notes you made along the way.

What emotions did this section trigger and what did it stir inside you?

What is true in your story? What does Scripture say about your situation?

_____

_____

_____

_____

_____

_____

_____

_____

_____

_____

_____

LEAN ON JESUS

But those who suffer he delivers in their suffering; he speaks to them in their affliction. (Job 36:15)

What does it look like to lean on Jesus as you enter those parts of your story that have caused you pain? Do you feel apprehensive, scared, unsure or relieved?

_____

_____

_____

_____

_____

_____

_____

_____

_____

_____

_____

_____

_____

INVEST IN PRAYER

Do not be anxious about anything, but in every situation, by prayer and petition, with thanksgiving, present your requests to God. (Philippians 4:6)

Pray for those areas where you may be stuck in anger, grief, anxiety, or hopelessness. Journal your prayers.

_____

_____

_____

_____

_____

_____

_____

_____

_____

_____

_____

_____

_____

_____

_____
_____
_____
_____
_____
_____

VALUE OTHERS

All the believers were one in heart and mind. No one claimed that any of their possessions was their own, but they shared everything they had. (Acts 4:32)

If you are doing this study as a group, get to know each other in order to become of "one in heart and mind." Commit to holding each other up in prayer and in deeds.

_____
_____
_____
_____
_____
_____
_____

Action Plan

_____
_____
_____
_____
_____
_____
_____

EMBRACE YOUR STORY

You, Lord, took up my case; you redeemed my life. (Lamentations 3:58)

If you were to pick out one positive story each for elementary, middle, and high school, what would those be?

_____

_____

_____

_____

_____

_____

_____

_____

_____

_____

_____

_____

_____

_____

_____

_____

_____

EXTRA NOTES:

_____

_____

_____

_____

_____

DIGEST & REFRAME

For those who are led by the Spirit of God are the children of God.
(Romans 8:14)

Expand on the pause and reflect questions and any additional notes you made along the way.

What emotions did this section trigger and what did it stir inside you?

What is true in your story? What does Scripture say about your situation?

_____

_____

_____

_____

_____

_____

_____

_____

_____

_____

_____

LEAN ON JESUS

But those who suffer he delivers in their suffering; he speaks to them in their affliction. (Job 36:15)

We can rely on our heavenly Father to fill the gaps left by our earthly parents. Have you considered that your parents may have received the same baggage they passed down to you? What are your thoughts on this?

_____

_____

_____

_____

_____

_____
_____
_____
_____
_____
_____
_____
_____
_____

INVEST IN PRAYER

Do not be anxious about anything, but in every situation, by prayer and petition, with thanksgiving, present your requests to God. (Philippians 4:6)

Pray to break the cycle of generational sins, negative patterns in your life, the life of your children and future generations. Be specific. Journal your prayers.

_____
_____
_____
_____
_____
_____
_____
_____
_____
_____
_____
_____
_____
_____
_____

_____
_____
_____
_____
_____
_____

VALUE OTHERS

All the believers were one in heart and mind. No one claimed that any of their possessions was their own, but they shared everything they had. (Acts 4:32)

Could your parent(s) or a family member use some encouragement? Send them a note, make a phone call, or buy them a gift.

_____
_____
_____
_____
_____
_____
_____

Action Plan

_____
_____
_____
_____
_____
_____
_____

EMBRACE YOUR STORY

You, Lord, took up my case; you redeemed my life. (Lamentations 3:58)

What were some important life lessons you learned while growing up?

_____

_____

_____

_____

_____

_____

_____

_____

_____

_____

_____

_____

_____

_____

_____

_____

_____

_____

_____

_____

EXTRA NOTES:

_____

_____

_____

_____

DIGEST & REFRAME

Then he said to them, "My soul is overwhelmed with sorrow to the point of death. Stay here and keep watch with me." (Matthew 26:38)

Expand on the pause and reflect questions and any additional notes you made along the way.

What emotions did this section trigger and what did it stir inside you?

What is true in your story? What does Scripture say about your situation?

_____

_____

_____

_____

_____

_____

_____

_____

_____

_____

_____

_____

LEAN ON JESUS

But those who suffer he delivers in their suffering; he speaks to them in their affliction. (Job 36:15)

As you lean on Jesus today, ask Him to speak to you in your affliction.

_____

_____

_____

_____

_____

_____

INVEST IN PRAYER

Do not be anxious about anything, but in every situation, by prayer and petition, with thanksgiving, present your requests to God. (Philippians 4:6)

If you do not have a trusted friend to do life with, ask God to show you who this could be. If you have a friend you can rely on, spend some time praying for them. Let this friend know how much you value them. Journal your prayers.

_____
_____
_____
_____
_____
_____

VALUE OTHERS

All the believers were one in heart and mind. No one claimed that any of their possessions was their own, but they shared everything they had. (Acts 4:32)

Send a note of support to someone who has experienced the loss of a loved one. Be mindful of birthdays and anniversaries.

_____
_____
_____
_____
_____
_____
_____

Action Plan

EMBRACE YOUR STORY

You, Lord, took up my case; you redeemed my life. (Lamentations 3:58)

What is a difficult situation you've managed to overcome?

_____

_____

_____

_____

_____

_____

_____

_____

_____

_____

_____

_____

_____

_____

_____

_____

_____

EXTRA NOTES:

_____

_____

_____

_____

_____

DIGEST & REFRAME

For God did not send his Son into the world to condemn the world, but to save the world through him. (John 3:17)

Expand on the pause and reflect questions and any additional notes you made along the way.

What emotions did this section trigger and what did it stir inside you?

What is true in your story? What does Scripture say about your situation?

_____

_____

_____

_____

_____

_____

_____

_____

_____

_____

_____

LEAN ON JESUS

But those who suffer he delivers in their suffering; he speaks to them in their affliction. (Job 36:15)

Do you believe Jesus can hold you up? Do you want Him to? What is the promise of Job 36:15?

_____

_____

_____

_____

_____

_____
_____
_____
_____
_____
_____
_____
_____
_____

INVEST IN PRAYER

Do not be anxious about anything, but in every situation, by prayer and petition, with thanksgiving, present your requests to God. (Philippians 4:6)

Offer up your prayers with thanksgiving, knowing that God hears all of your requests. Journal your prayers.

_____
_____
_____
_____
_____
_____
_____
_____
_____
_____
_____
_____
_____
_____

_____
_____
_____
_____
_____
_____

VALUE OTHERS

All the believers were one in heart and mind. No one claimed that any of their possessions was their own, but they shared everything they had. (Acts 4:32)

As believers, we must care for both the mother and the unborn child with unity of heart and mind. Do you hold firm beliefs about the sanctity of life, or are you undecided about your stance on abortion? If you struggle in this area, ask God to speak to you and give you wisdom as you wrestle in this.

_____
_____
_____
_____
_____
_____
_____

Action Plan

_____
_____
_____
_____
_____
_____

EMBRACE YOUR STORY

You, Lord, took up my case; you redeemed my life. (Lamentations 3:58)

Describe a loved one and the qualities that make them unique.

_____

_____

_____

_____

_____

_____

_____

_____

_____

_____

_____

_____

_____

_____

_____

_____

_____

_____

AFTER SOME TIME:

_____

_____

_____

_____

_____

2

What Are You Seeking?

We are all in search of something. We seek healing, truth, God, revenge, love, money, purpose, wisdom, or status. Throughout my young adult life, I have spent more time seeking rather than living. Seeking can be a negative pattern if it keeps you stuck, just as I was in the search for my biological father.

DIGEST & REFRAME

Though my father and mother forsake me, the LORD will receive me.
(Psalm 27:10)

Expand on the pause and reflect questions and any additional notes you made along the way.

What emotions did this section trigger and what did it stir inside you?

What is true in your story? What does Scripture say about your situation?

_____

_____

_____

_____

_____

_____

_____

_____

_____

_____

LEAN ON JESUS

Call to me and I will answer you and tell you great and unsearchable things you do not know. (Jeremiah 33:3)

Do you struggle to believe that God is the perfect Father who wants to hear from you? How does this keep you from fully leaning on Jesus? Write about this struggle.

_____

_____

_____

_____

_____

_____

_____

_____

_____

_____

_____

_____

_____

_____

INVEST IN PRAYER

Rejoice always, pray continually, give thanks in all circumstances; for this is God's will for you in Christ Jesus. (1 Thessalonians 5:16-18)

Pray for the faith to trust God as the perfect Father who always has your best interests at heart—even when you can't understand your circumstances. Journal your prayers.

_____

_____

_____

_____

_____

_____

_____

_____

_____

_____

_____

_____

_____

_____

_____

_____

_____

_____

VALUE OTHERS

Religion that our Father accepts as pure and faultless is this: to look after the orphans and widows in their distress and to keep oneself from being polluted by the world. (James 1:27)

Identify the orphans in your church. For the sake of valuing others can we see an orphan as a person who is new to the church community with no family connections. What can you do to welcome them—as a part of the family of believers?

_____

_____

_____

_____

_____

_____

_____

Action Plan

_____

_____

_____

_____

_____

_____

EMBRACE YOUR STORY

I know that my redeemer lives, and that in the end he will stand on the earth.
(Job 19:25)

Write about a family secret. How has this secret impacted your life?

EXTRA NOTES:

DIGEST & REFRAME

May the God of hope fill you with all joy and peace as you trust in him, so that you may overflow with hope by the power of the Holy Spirit. (Romans 15:13)

Expand on the pause and reflect questions and any additional notes you made along the way.

What emotions did this section trigger and what did it stir inside you?

What is true in your story? What does Scripture say about your situation?

_____

_____

_____

_____

_____

_____

_____

_____

_____

_____

_____

LEAN ON JESUS

Call to me and I will answer you and tell you great and unsearchable things you do not know. (Jeremiah 33:3)

Ask God for insight into areas of your life where you may be stuck.

_____

_____

_____

_____

_____

_____

_____

_____

_____

_____

_____

_____

_____

_____

_____

INVEST IN PRAYER

Rejoice always, pray continually, give thanks in all circumstances; for this is God's will for you in Christ Jesus. (1 Thessalonians 5:16-18)

Pray for friends and family members who are seeking. Journal your prayers.

_____

_____

_____

_____

_____

_____

_____

_____

_____

_____

_____

_____

_____

_____

_____

_____

_____

_____

_____

_____

_____

_____

VALUE OTHERS

Religion that our Father accepts as pure and faultless is this: to look after the orphans and widows in their distress and to keep oneself from being polluted by the world. (James 1:27)

Are there widows in your church that could use some looking after? Do they need help with home repairs or yard work? Organize a work day to help meet these needs and include the youth group in these projects.

_____

_____

_____

_____

_____

_____

_____

_____

_____

Action Plan

_____

_____

_____

_____

_____

_____

EMBRACE YOUR STORY

I know that my redeemer lives, and that in the end he will stand on the earth.
(Job 19:25)

What are your dreams for your life. Don't hold back. Sometimes God places dreams in your heart that will lead you to His purpose.

_____

_____

_____

_____

_____

_____

_____

_____

_____

_____

_____

_____

_____

_____

_____

_____

_____

_____

EXTRA NOTES:

_____

_____

_____

_____

_____

DIGEST & REFRAME

Take delight in the LORD, and he will give you the desires of your heart.
(Psalm 37:3)

Expand on the pause and reflect questions and any additional notes you made along the way.

What emotions did this section trigger and what did it stir inside you?

What is true in your story? What does Scripture say about your situation?

_____

_____

_____

_____

_____

_____

_____

_____

_____

_____

LEAN ON JESUS

Call to me and I will answer you and tell you great and unsearchable things you do not know. (Jeremiah 33:3)

What are the most common distractions you face on a day-to-day basis that keep you from spending time with Jesus? I keep a pen and paper handy for when distractions come, such as my to-do list, and I write them down. This gets it out of my head and allows me to get back to my time with Jesus. Write some solutions for when distractions appear.

_____

_____

_____

_____

_____
_____
_____
_____
_____
_____
_____
_____

INVEST IN PRAYER

Rejoice always, pray continually, give thanks in all circumstances; for this is
God's will for you in Christ Jesus. (1 Thessalonians 5:16-18)

Express gratitude for the circumstances you are experiencing today. I
realize this can be extremely difficult. I struggle with giving thanks in ALL
circumstances as well. Journal your prayers.

_____
_____
_____
_____
_____
_____
_____
_____
_____
_____
_____
_____
_____

_____

_____

_____

_____

_____

VALUE OTHERS

Religion that our Father accepts as pure and faultless is this: to look after the orphans and widows in their distress and to keep oneself from being polluted by the world. (James 1:27)

What in your day-to-day life is polluting your mind? How can you combat the negativity in the world and create a positive impact on others?

_____

_____

_____

_____

_____

_____

_____

_____

_____

_____

_____

Action Plan

_____

_____

_____

_____

_____

_____

EMBRACE YOUR STORY

I know that my redeemer lives, and that in the end he will stand on the earth.
(Job 19:25)

Describe the moment a dream or longing became reality.

_____

_____

_____

_____

_____

_____

_____

_____

_____

_____

_____

_____

_____

_____

_____

_____

_____

EXTRA NOTES:

_____

_____

_____

_____

_____

DIGEST & REFRAME

I am the LORD, the God of all mankind. Is anything too hard for me?
(Jeremiah 32:27)

Expand on the pause and reflect questions and any additional notes you made along the way.

What emotions did this section trigger and what did it stir inside you?

What is true in your story? What does Scripture say about your situation?

_____

_____

_____

_____

_____

_____

_____

_____

_____

_____

_____

LEAN ON JESUS

Call to me and I will answer you and tell you great and unsearchable things you
do not know. (Jeremiah 33:3)

God sent His one and only Son to die on the cross for you so that you may have a personal relationship with Him. God made the impossible possible through Jesus—all you have to do is call out to Him. How often do you call out to Jesus?

_____

_____

_____

_____

_____

INVEST IN PRAYER

Rejoice always, pray continually, give thanks in all circumstances; for this is God's will for you in Christ Jesus. (1 Thessalonians 5:16-18)

What is a prayer that you believe will never be answered - a prayer for something you believe is impossible? Journal your prayers.

_____

_____

_____

_____

_____

_____

VALUE OTHERS

Religion that our Father accepts as pure and faultless is this: to look after the orphans and widows in their distress and to keep oneself from being polluted by the world. (James 1:27)

What steps can you take to make a difference in the lives of foster children in your community?

_____

_____

_____

_____

_____

_____

_____

_____

Action Plan

_____

_____

_____

_____

_____

_____

_____

EMBRACE YOUR STORY

I know that my redeemer lives, and that in the end he will stand on the earth.
(Job 19:25)

What did you long for as a child?

_____

_____

_____

_____

_____

_____

_____

_____

_____

_____

_____

_____

_____

_____

_____

_____

_____

_____

EXTRA NOTES:

_____

_____

_____

_____

_____

DIGEST & REFRAME

Do nothing out of selfish ambition or vain deceit. Rather, in humility value others above yourselves, not looking to your own interests but each of you to the interests of the others. (Philippians 2:3-4)

Expand on the pause and reflect questions and any additional notes you made along the way.

What emotions did this section trigger and what did it stir inside you?

What is true in your story? What does Scripture say about your situation?

_____

_____

_____

_____

_____

_____

_____

_____

_____

_____

LEAN ON JESUS

Call to me and I will answer you and tell you great and unsearchable things you do not know. (Jeremiah 33:3)

Jesus sees you. He sees your pain, needs and sufferings. Do you believe this? What do you base your answer on?

_____

_____

_____

_____

_____

_____

_____

_____

_____

_____

_____

_____

_____

_____

INVEST IN PRAYER

Rejoice always, pray continually, give thanks in all circumstances; for this is God's will for you in Christ Jesus. (1 Thessalonians 5:16-18)

Pray for someone who has abandoned or betrayed you. Journal your prayers.

_____

_____

_____

_____

_____

_____

_____

_____

_____

_____

_____

_____

_____

_____

_____

_____
_____
_____
_____
_____

VALUE OTHERS

Religion that our Father accepts as pure and faultless is this: to look after the
orphans and widows in their distress and to keep oneself from being polluted
by the world. (James 1:27)

**Is there someone in your life that pours wisdom and life experiences into
you? Do you pour into a younger person? How would being mentored and/or
mentoring someone fit into your life?**

_____
_____
_____
_____
_____
_____

Action Plan

_____
_____
_____
_____
_____
_____
_____

EMBRACE YOUR STORY

I know that my redeemer lives, and that in the end he will stand on the earth.
(Job 19:25)

Describe a time you went out on a limb for someone.

AFTER SOME TIME:

3

Who Are You?

You are God's masterpiece. There is no name given to you or anything you identify with that overrides who God created you to be. You have a specific purpose and all your life experiences, no matter what they are, can fulfill God's plan for you. These experiences, along with life's struggles, shape us and make us unique. It all contributes to the beautiful and fruitful lives God wants us to live.

DIGEST & REFRAME

I praise you because I am fearfully and wonderfully made; your works are wonderful, I know that full well. (Psalm 139:14)

Expand on the pause and reflect questions and any additional notes you made along the way.

What emotions did this section trigger and what did it stir inside you?

What is true in your story? What does Scripture say about your situation?

_____

_____

_____

_____

_____

_____

_____

_____

_____

_____

_____

LEAN ON JESUS

Yet to all who did receive him, to those who believed in his name, he gave the right to become children of God. (John 1:12)

You are born of God; you are His child. You bear His image (Genesis 1:27). Sit with this for a few minutes. Don't dismiss it. How does today's verse speak to you?

_____

_____

_____

_____

_____

_____
_____
_____
_____
_____
_____
_____
_____
_____

INVEST IN PRAYER

Devote yourselves to prayer, being watchful and thankful. (Colossians 4:2)

Prayer and gratitude intertwine. Do your prayers focus solely on requests, without giving equal attention to gratitude? Ask God to fill you with a spirit of gratitude. Journal your prayers.

_____
_____
_____
_____
_____
_____
_____
_____
_____
_____
_____
_____
_____
_____
_____
_____

_____
_____
_____
_____
_____
_____

VALUE OTHERS

Therefore encourage one another and build each other up, just as in fact you are doing. (1 Thessalonians 5:11)

Offer encouragement to a friend who is facing challenges. How can you help in building them up?

_____
_____
_____
_____
_____
_____
_____

Action Plan

_____
_____
_____
_____
_____
_____

EMBRACE YOUR STORY

Do not fear, for I have redeemed you; I have summoned you by name; you are mine. (Isaiah 43:1)

Who in the Bible can you relate to the most? What is it about them you identify with?

_____

_____

_____

_____

_____

_____

_____

_____

_____

_____

_____

_____

_____

_____

_____

_____

EXTRA NOTES:

_____

_____

_____

_____

DIGEST & REFRAME

Before I was born the LORD called me; from my mother's womb he has spoken my name. (Isaiah 49:1)

Expand on the pause and reflect questions and any additional notes you made along the way.

What emotions did this section trigger and what did it stir inside you?

What is true in your story? What does Scripture say about your situation?

_____

_____

_____

_____

_____

_____

_____

_____

_____

_____

_____

LEAN ON JESUS

Yet to all who did receive him, to those who believed in his name, he gave the right to become children of God. (John 1:12)

As a Father, God knows everything about you. What can you do to deepen your personal knowledge of God?

_____

_____

_____

_____

_____

_____
_____
_____
_____
_____
_____
_____
_____
_____

INVEST IN PRAYER

Devote yourselves to prayer, being watchful and thankful. (Colossians 4:2)

Seek God's help in forgiving those who have used hurtful words against you. Journal your prayers.

_____
_____
_____
_____
_____
_____
_____
_____
_____
_____
_____
_____
_____
_____
_____
_____
_____

_____
_____
_____
_____
_____
_____

VALUE OTHERS

Therefore encourage one another and build each other up, just as in fact you are doing. (1 Thessalonians 5:11)

Seek forgiveness from those you have hurt with your words.

_____
_____
_____
_____
_____
_____
_____
_____

Action Plan

_____
_____
_____
_____
_____
_____
_____

EMBRACE YOUR STORY

Do not fear, for I have redeemed you; I have summoned you by name; you are mine. (Isaiah 43:1)

Describe a situation that has caused you to see yourself as flawed.

_____

_____

_____

_____

_____

_____

_____

_____

_____

_____

_____

_____

_____

_____

_____

_____

_____

EXTRA NOTES:

_____

_____

_____

_____

_____

DIGEST & REFRAME

For we are God's handiwork, created in Christ Jesus to do good works, which God prepared in advance for us to do. (Ephesians 2:10)

Expand on the pause and reflect questions and any additional notes you made along the way.

What emotions did this section trigger and what did it stir inside you?

What is true in your story? What does Scripture say about your situation?

_____

_____

_____

_____

_____

_____

_____

_____

_____

_____

LEAN ON JESUS

Yet to all who did receive him, to those who believed in his name, he gave the right to become children of God. (John 1:12)

As we surrender our life to God we must learn to take "every thought captive and make it obedient to Christ" (2 Corinthians 10:5). Are there specific thoughts you struggle with?

_____

_____

_____

_____

_____

_____
_____
_____
_____
_____
_____
_____
_____
_____

INVEST IN PRAYER

Devote yourselves to prayer, being watchful and thankful. (Colossians 4:2)

Ask God to show you how He sees you in Christ. Journal your prayers.

_____
_____
_____
_____
_____
_____
_____
_____
_____
_____
_____
_____
_____
_____
_____
_____

_____
_____
_____
_____
_____
_____

VALUE OTHERS

Therefore encourage one another and build each other up, just as in fact you
are doing. (1 Thessalonians 5:11)

How do you treat those who differ from you? Do you look down on those
you think are less fortunate or different from you? Be aware of your personal
biases. Ask God to reveal these to you. Who comes to mind after reading this?
Is there something you can do for this person?

_____
_____
_____
_____
_____
_____

Action Plan

_____
_____
_____
_____
_____
_____

EMBRACE YOUR STORY

Do not fear, for I have redeemed you; I have summoned you by name; you are mine. (Isaiah 43:1)

What life event has strengthened your connection with God the most?

_____
_____
_____
_____
_____
_____
_____
_____
_____
_____
_____
_____
_____
_____
_____
_____

EXTRA NOTES:

_____
_____
_____
_____
_____

DIGEST & REFRAME

Yet you, LORD, are our Father. We are the clay, you are the potter; we are all the work of your hand. (Isaiah 64:8)

Expand on the pause and reflect questions and any additional notes you made along the way.

What emotions did this section trigger and what did it stir inside you?

What is true in your story? What does Scripture say about your situation?

_____

_____

_____

_____

_____

_____

_____

_____

_____

_____

_____

LEAN ON JESUS

Yet to all who did receive him, to those who believed in his name, he gave the right to become children of God. (John 1:12)

I used to think that my gift of empathy was a curse, because I didn't know what to do with it. As the clay in the potter's hand, do you believe you have been given a gift or a curse? Sit with your thoughts on this, then journal what comes to you.

_____

_____

_____

_____

_____

INVEST IN PRAYER

Devote yourselves to prayer, being watchful and thankful. (Colossians 4:2)

Pray for insight into how your suffering may influence your behavior. Do you self-loath or become critical of others? Journal your prayers.

_____

_____

_____

_____

_____

_____

VALUE OTHERS

Therefore encourage one another and build each other up, just as in fact you are doing. (1 Thessalonians 5:11)

Who do you know that needs to hear the truth of who they are-how God sees them? Start praying for them. Ask God for an opportunity to speak truth into their life.

_____

_____

_____

_____

_____

_____

_____

_____

_____

_____

_____

_____

_____

Action Plan

EMBRACE YOUR STORY

Do not fear, for I have redeemed you; I have summoned you by name; you are mine. (Isaiah 43:1)

What makes you, YOU? Write about your unique qualities, gifts, and talents.

_____
_____
_____
_____
_____
_____
_____
_____
_____
_____
_____
_____
_____
_____
_____
_____
_____
_____

EXTRA NOTES:

_____
_____
_____
_____
_____

DIGEST & REFRAME

Therefore, if anyone is in Christ, the new creation has come: The old is gone, the new is here! (2 Corinthians 5:17)

Expand on the pause and reflect questions and any additional notes you made along the way.

What emotions did this section trigger and what did it stir inside you?

What is true in your story? What does Scripture say about your situation?

_____

_____

_____

_____

_____

_____

_____

_____

_____

_____

_____

LEAN ON JESUS

Yet to all who did receive him, to those who believed in his name, he gave the right to become children of God. (John 1:12)

Write some life-giving names you would love for your heavenly Father to call you as His child. Ask Jesus, which one of these names do you want to speak over me today? Listen and journal what you hear.

_____

_____

_____

_____

_____

INVEST IN PRAYER

Devote yourselves to prayer, being watchful and thankful. (Colossians 4:2)

Try using different names for God when you pray. Journal your prayers.

_____
_____
_____
_____
_____

VALUE OTHERS

Therefore encourage one another and build each other up, just as in fact you are doing. (1 Thessalonians 5:11)

Is there someone that comes to mind whom you need to encourage and build up instead of tearing them down?

_____
_____
_____
_____
_____
_____
_____
_____

Action Plan

_____
_____
_____
_____
_____
_____
_____

EMBRACE YOUR STORY

Do not fear, for I have redeemed you; I have summoned you by name; you are mine. (Isaiah 43:1)

God brings people into our lives to help us see the truth and heal. If you're struggling with negative names, ask a friend to speak the truth of how they see you through Christ. Ask them to name the redeeming qualities your life exudes. Write these down.

_____

_____

_____

_____

_____

_____

_____

_____

_____

_____

_____

_____

_____

_____

_____

_____

_____

AFTER SOME TIME:

_____

_____

_____

_____

_____

4

What Are You Hiding?

Have you ever shared a secret and then felt relieved to get it off your chest? This is evidence of how heavy secrets can be. Sometimes it is not only what we are hiding, but from whom. When Adam and Eve sinned, their first response was to hide from God. Unconfessed sin will always put a wedge between God and us. Our culture has become more tolerant and desensitized to sin. This doesn't mean God has. Repentance and confession are necessary in addressing sin. In 1 John 1:9 we have a solid promise that, "If we confess our sins, he is faithful and just and will forgive us our sins and purify us from all unrighteousness."

DIGEST & REFRAME

For all have sinned and fall short of the glory of God, and all are justified freely by his grace through the redemption that came by Christ Jesus.
(Romans 3:23-24)

Expand on the pause and reflect questions and any additional notes you made along the way.

What emotions did this section trigger and what did it stir inside you?

What is true in your story? What does Scripture say about your situation?

_____

_____

_____

_____

_____

_____

_____

_____

_____

_____

LEAN ON JESUS

But you, man of God, flee from all this, and pursue righteousness, godliness, faith, love, endurance and gentleness. Fight the good fight of the faith.
(1 Timothy 6:11-12)

What are you to pursue and what is God asking of you? What does this look like in your day-to-day life?

_____

_____

_____

_____

_____

_____

_____

_____

_____

_____

_____

_____

_____

_____

_____

INVEST IN PRAYER

Watch and pray so that you will not fall into temptation. The spirit is willing, but the flesh is weak. (Matthew 26:41)

Ask God to reveal any if people knew secrets that are keeping you. Confess those and ask for forgiveness where needed. Journal your prayers.

_____

_____

_____

_____

_____

_____

_____

_____

_____

_____

_____

_____

_____

_____

_____

_____

_____

_____

_____

_____

VALUE OTHERS

A new command I give you: Love one another. As I have loved you, so you must love one another. (John 13:34)

Do you know someone that has retreated socially? Connect with them and let them know they are missed.

_____

_____

_____

_____

_____

_____

_____

_____

Action Plan

_____

_____

_____

_____

_____

EMBRACE YOUR STORY

Praise the LORD, my soul, and forget not all his benefits-who forgives all your sins and heals all your diseases, who redeems your life from the pit and crowns you with love and compassion, who satisfied your desires with good things so that your youth is renewed like the eagle's. (Psalm 103:2-5)

What do you wish people knew about you?

_____

_____

_____

_____

_____

_____

_____

_____

_____

_____

_____

_____

_____

_____

_____

_____

_____

_____

_____

EXTRA NOTES:

_____

_____

_____

_____

_____

DAY 2: DOMESTIC VIOLENCE

DIGEST & REFRAME

And my God will meet all your needs according to the riches of his glory in
Christ Jesus. (Philippians 4:19)

Expand on the pause and reflect questions and any additional notes you made
along the way.

What emotions did this section trigger and what did it stir inside you?

What is true in your story? What does Scripture say about your situation?

_____

_____

_____

_____

_____

_____

_____

_____

_____

_____

_____

LEAN ON JESUS

But you, man of God, flee from all this, and pursue righteousness, godliness,
faith, love, endurance and gentleness. Fight the good fight of the faith. (1
Timothy 6:11-12)

Will you choose to fight the good fight and stand strong in your faith? How
does leaning on Jesus daily prepare you for this battle?

_____

_____

_____

_____

_____

_____

_____

_____

_____

_____

_____

_____

_____

INVEST IN PRAYER

Watch and pray so that you will not fall into temptation. The spirit is willing, but the flesh is weak. (Matthew 26:41)

Pray for women who are facing abuse and for those whom are seeking a fresh start. Journal your prayers.

_____

_____

_____

_____

_____

_____

_____

_____

_____

_____

_____

_____

_____

_____

VALUE OTHERS

A new command I give you: Love one another. As I have loved you, so you must love one another. (John 13:34)

How can you best support your local women's shelter or pregnancy care center?

Action Plan

EMBRACE YOUR STORY

Praise the LORD, my soul, and forget not all his benefits-who forgives all your sins and heals all your diseases, who redeems your life from the pit and crowns you with love and compassion, who satisfied your desires with good things so that your youth is renewed like the eagle's. (Psalm 103:2-5)

If you were as free as an eagle, what heights would you soar to?

_____
_____
_____
_____
_____
_____
_____
_____
_____
_____
_____
_____
_____
_____
_____
_____
_____

EXTRA NOTES:

_____
_____
_____
_____
_____

DIGEST & REFRAME

Do not judge, or you too will be judged. (Matthew 7:1)

Expand on the pause and reflect questions and any additional notes you made along the way.

What emotions did this section trigger and what did it stir inside you?

What is true in your story? What does Scripture say about your situation?

_____
_____
_____
_____
_____
_____
_____
_____
_____
_____
_____

LEAN ON JESUS

But you, man of God, flee from all this, and pursue righteousness, godliness, faith, love, endurance and gentleness. Fight the good fight of the faith. (1 Timothy 6:11-12)

We never have to fake it with Jesus. He knows. Thank Him for loving you regardless of anything you've thought or done.

_____
_____
_____
_____
_____

INVEST IN PRAYER

Watch and pray so that you will not fall into temptation. The spirit is willing, but the flesh is weak. (Matthew 26:41)

Are you faking it, going through the motions? Pray for the courage to take off your mask and unveil your authentic self to your circle of friends. Journal your prayers.

_____
_____
_____
_____
_____
_____

VALUE OTHERS

A new command I give you: Love one another. As I have loved you, so you must love one another. (John 13:34)

Reach out to someone you have misjudged and get to know them.

_____
_____
_____
_____
_____
_____
_____
_____

Action Plan

_____
_____
_____
_____
_____
_____

EMBRACE YOUR STORY

Praise the LORD, my soul, and forget not all his benefits-who forgives all your sins and heals all your diseases, who redeems your life from the pit and crowns you with love and compassion, who satisfied your desires with good things so that your youth is renewed like the eagle's. (Psalm 103:2-5)

What parts of your story do you feel alone in? Be specific.

EXTRA NOTES:

DAY 4: LIFE IS TOUGH

DIGEST & REFRAME

If we confess our sins, he is faithful and just and will forgive us our sins and purify us from all unrighteousness. (1 John 1:9)

Expand on the pause and reflect questions and any additional notes you made along the way.

What emotions did this section trigger and what did it stir inside you?

What is true in your story? What does Scripture say about your situation?

_____

_____

_____

_____

_____

_____

_____

_____

_____

_____

_____

LEAN ON JESUS

But you, man of God, flee from all this, and pursue righteousness, godliness, faith, love, endurance and gentleness. Fight the good fight of the faith.
(1 Timothy 6:11-12)

In difficult times, what measures can you take to prevent yourself from slipping?

_____

_____

_____

_____

_____

_____
_____
_____
_____
_____
_____
_____
_____
_____

INVEST IN PRAYER

Watch and pray so that you will not fall into temptation. The spirit is willing, but the flesh is weak. (Matthew 26:41)

Ask God to show you where your foundation, thoughts, or personal beliefs are weak and need to be strengthened with the truth. Journal your prayers.

_____
_____
_____
_____
_____
_____
_____
_____
_____
_____
_____
_____
_____
_____

_____
_____
_____
_____
_____
_____

VALUE OTHERS

A new command I give you: Love one another. As I have loved you, so you must love one another. (John 13:34)

Show support to single mothers in your community. What can you do for one single mom?

_____
_____
_____
_____
_____
_____
_____
_____

Action Plan

_____
_____
_____
_____
_____
_____

EMBRACE YOUR STORY

Praise the LORD, my soul, and forget not all his benefits-who forgives all your sins and heals all your diseases, who redeems your life from the pit and crowns you with love and compassion, who satisfied your desires with good things so that your youth is renewed like the eagle's. (Psalm 103:2-5)

Write a praise to the Lord from the depth of your soul.

_____

_____

_____

_____

_____

_____

_____

_____

_____

_____

_____

_____

_____

_____

_____

_____

_____

EXTRA NOTES:

_____

_____

_____

_____

DIGEST & REFRAME

If we confess our sins, he is faithful and just and will forgive us our sins and purify us from all unrighteousness. (1 John 1:9)

Expand on the pause and reflect questions and any additional notes you made along the way.

What emotions did this section trigger and what did it stir inside you?

What is true in your story? What does Scripture say about your situation?

_____
_____
_____
_____
_____
_____
_____
_____
_____
_____
_____
_____

LEAN ON JESUS

But you, man of God, flee from all this, and pursue righteousness, godliness, faith, love, endurance and gentleness. Fight the good fight of the faith. (1 Timothy 6:11-12)

Jesus intentionally went to the place where the Samaritan woman was going to be. Think about a time when Jesus met you unexpectedly. What does this say about his love towards you?

_____
_____
_____
_____
_____

_____

_____

_____

_____

_____

_____

_____

_____

INVEST IN PRAYER

Watch and pray so that you will not fall into temptation. The spirit is willing, but the flesh is weak. (Matthew 26:41)

Do you judge certain sins or behaviors in others, yet let those you struggle with slide? Be careful of judging someone who struggles differently than you do. We all fall short; some of our shortcomings are not as clear as others. Pray over your shortcomings and for the ability to extend grace towards others in their shortcomings. Journal your prayers.

_____

_____

_____

_____

_____

_____

_____

_____

_____

_____

_____

_____

_____

_____

_____

_____

_____

VALUE OTHERS

A new command I give you: Love one another. As I have loved you, so you must love one another. (John 13:34)

Go out of your way to share the good news with someone in your community.

_____

_____

_____

_____

_____

_____

_____

_____

Action Plan

_____

_____

_____

_____

_____

_____

_____

EMBRACE YOUR STORY

Praise the LORD, my soul, and forget not all his benefits-who forgives all your sins and heals all your diseases, who redeems your life from the pit and crowns you with love and compassion, who satisfied your desires with good things so that your youth is renewed like the eagle's. (Psalm 103:2-5)

What activities ignite your passion and make you feel alive and energized?

_____

_____

_____

_____

_____

_____

_____

_____

_____

_____

_____

_____

_____

_____

_____

_____

_____

AFTER SOME TIME:

_____

_____

_____

_____

_____

5

How Do You Process?

God's accomplishes his finest work in the valley, if we allow it. It is with His help that we can climb up from the deepest of canyons. There are moments when God carries us out completely, and others when we walk with him step by step, always keeping our gaze fixed on Him. I don't understand it, and would rather avoid suffering altogether BUT my faith and love for God is even richer because of my sufferings.

DIGEST & REFRAME

Praise be to the God and Father of our Lord Jesus Christ, the Father of compassion and the God of all comfort, who comforts us in all our troubles, so that we can comfort those in any trouble with the comfort we ourselves receive from God. (2 Corinthians 1:3)

Expand on the pause and reflect questions and any additional notes you made along the way.

What emotions did this section trigger and what did it stir inside you?

What is true in your story? What does Scripture say about your situation?

_____

_____

_____

_____

_____

_____

_____

_____

_____

LEAN ON JESUS

My help comes from the LORD, the Maker of heaven and earth. (Psalm 121:2)

When faced with a difficult situation, do you fill yourself with stuff instead of the Holy Spirit? If you are filling yourself with those things that will leave you empty, what steps can you take to change this?

_____

_____

_____

_____

_____

INVEST IN PRAYER

In the same way, the Spirit helps us in our weakness. We do not know what we ought to pray for, but the Spirit himself intercedes for us through wordless groans. (Romans 8:26)

Pray for those who are struggling with finding meaning in their life. If this is you right now, reach out and seek the support you need to get through this tough season. Don't do this alone. Find someone in whom you can confide with who will offer the help you need. There are professionals that can give you the tools to process through your situation. Journal your prayers.

_____

_____

_____

_____

_____

_____

VALUE OTHERS

In everything I did, I showed you that by this kind of hard work we must help the weak, remembering the words the Lord Jesus himself said: It is more blessed to give than to receive. (Acts 20:35)

We can give others our time, prayer, and a listening ear. Who in your life needs this right now?

_____

_____

_____

_____

_____

_____

_____

_____   *Action Plan*

_____

_____

_____

_____

_____

_____

_____

EMBRACE YOUR STORY

In your unfailing love you will lead the people you have redeemed.
(Exodus 15:13)

How do you like to spend your leisure time? What about this activity do you find enjoyable?

_____

_____

_____

_____

_____

_____

_____

_____

_____

_____

_____

_____

_____

_____

_____

_____

_____

_____

EXTRA NOTES:

_____

_____

_____

_____

_____

DAY 2: TEARS THAT SAVE

DIGEST & REFRAME

Jesus wept. (John 11:35)

Expand on the pause and reflect questions and any additional notes you made along the way.

What emotions did this section trigger and what did it stir inside you?

What is true in your story? What does Scripture say about your situation?

_____

_____

_____

_____

_____

_____

_____

_____

_____

_____

_____

_____

_____

LEAN ON JESUS

My help comes from the LORD, the Maker of heaven and earth. (Psalm 121:2)

Pay attention to those people or things you heavily rely on to help you. Do you go to those who have a genuine concern over your life or those that help you forget your problems? Explain your actions.

_____

_____

_____

_____

_____

INVEST IN PRAYER

In the same way, the Spirit helps us in our weakness. We do not know what we ought to pray for, but the Spirit himself intercedes for us through wordless groans. (Romans 8:26)

In times of deep suffering do you allow the Spirit to intercede for you? Sit in silence during your prayer time today and allow the Spirit to move in you. Journal your prayers.

_____

_____

_____

_____

_____

_____

VALUE OTHERS

In everything I did, I showed you that by this kind of hard work we must help the weak, remembering the words the Lord Jesus himself said: It is more blessed to give than to receive. (Acts 20:35)

How can you contribute to a non-profit organization that aligns with your values?

_____

_____

_____

_____

_____

_____

_____

_____

_____

_____

_____

_____

_____

_____

_____

_____

Action Plan

EMBRACE YOUR STORY

In your unfailing love you will lead the people you have redeemed.
(Exodus 15:13)

Write about a time someone shed tears for you? How did you feel about this?

_____

_____

_____

_____

_____

_____

_____

_____

_____

_____

_____

_____

_____

_____

_____

_____

_____

EXTRA NOTES:

_____

_____

_____

_____

_____

DAY 3: JUST HOLD ON

DIGEST & REFRAME

The King will reply, Truly I tell you, whatever you did for one of the least of these brothers and sisters of mine, you did for me. (Matthew 25:40)

Expand on the pause and reflect questions and any additional notes you made along the way.

What emotions did this section trigger and what did it stir inside you?

What is true in your story? What does Scripture say about your situation?

_____

_____

_____

_____

_____

_____

_____

_____

_____

_____

_____

_____

LEAN ON JESUS

My help comes from the LORD, the Maker of heaven and earth. (Psalm 121:2)

How do your actions in life show that your help is from the Lord? What can you do to lean on Jesus in all things with wholeheartedness?

_____

_____

_____

_____

_____

_____

_____

_____
_____
_____
_____
_____
_____
_____
_____

INVEST IN PRAYER

In the same way, the Spirit helps us in our weakness. We do not know what we ought to pray for, but the Spirit himself intercedes for us through wordless groans. (Romans 8:26)

Trust the Holy Spirit to be your help in times of weakness. Journal your prayers.

_____
_____
_____
_____
_____
_____
_____
_____
_____
_____
_____
_____

_____
_____
_____
_____
_____
_____

VALUE OTHERS

In everything I did, I showed you that by this kind of hard work we must help the weak, remembering the words the Lord Jesus himself said: It is more blessed to give than to receive. (Acts 20:35)

Connect with the youth pastor of your church. Ask what the primary needs are among the students and how you can help meet some of them.

_____
_____
_____
_____
_____
_____
_____

Action Plan

_____
_____
_____
_____
_____
_____

EMBRACE YOUR STORY

In your unfailing love you will lead the people you have redeemed.
(Exodus 15:13)

Write about your ideal place to unwind.

_____

_____

_____

_____

_____

_____

_____

_____

_____

_____

_____

_____

_____

_____

_____

_____

_____

_____

_____

EXTRA NOTES:

_____

_____

_____

_____

_____

DIGEST & REFRAME

When the devil had finished all this tempting, he left him until an opportune time. (Luke 4:13)

Expand on the pause and reflect questions and any additional notes you made along the way.

What emotions did this section trigger and what did it stir inside you?

What is true in your story? What does Scripture say about your situation?

_____

_____

_____

_____

_____

_____

_____

_____

_____

_____

_____

LEAN ON JESUS

My help comes from the LORD, the Maker of heaven and earth. (Psalm 121:2)

Do you believe that God is good even when harm comes your way? Have you considered that the greatest harm God keeps us from is eternal, not of this world? Journal your thoughts.

_____

_____

_____

_____

_____

_____

_____

_____
_____
_____
_____
_____
_____
_____
_____
_____

INVEST IN PRAYER

In the same way, the Spirit helps us in our weakness. We do not know what we ought to pray for, but the Spirit himself intercedes for us through wordless groans. (Romans 8:26)

Pray for teens in your community. They are fighting a battle beyond our awareness. Pray for those you know by name. Journal your prayers.

_____
_____
_____
_____
_____
_____
_____
_____
_____
_____
_____
_____

_____

_____

_____

_____

_____

VALUE OTHERS

In everything I did, I showed you that by this kind of hard work we must help the weak, remembering the words the Lord Jesus himself said: It is more blessed to give than to receive. (Acts 20:35)

When my daughter was going through a tough time, I asked adults from our small group and her Sunday school teachers to write her notes of encouragement. I folded each note and put them inside balloons. She enjoyed popping the bouquet of balloons to find the mystery they held inside. This blessed her teenage heart as she read the words of encouragement and love that came from someone other than mom. Our teens need adults to speak life into them. Does a specific teen come to mind? How can you bless them this week?

_____

_____

_____

_____

_____   *Action Plan*

_____

_____

_____

_____

_____

_____

_____

EMBRACE YOUR STORY

In your unfailing love you will lead the people you have redeemed.
(Exodus 15:13)

Write a Biblical life-affirming proclamation over your life. Place it somewhere you can see it throughout the day. I used to write memory verses on 3x5 index cards and keep them in my pocket or desk at work. Throughout the day, I would pull it out and read it. This helped to set my mind on things above (Colossians 3:2).

EXTRA NOTES:

DAY 5: TEARS THAT HEAL

DIGEST & REFRAME

With the tongue we praise our Lord and Father, and with it we curse human beings, who have been made in God's likeness. Out of the same mouth come praise and cursing. My brothers and sisters, this should not be. (James 3:9-10)

Expand on the pause and reflect questions and any additional notes you made along the way.

What emotions did this section trigger and what did it stir inside you?

What is true in your story? What does Scripture say about your situation?

_____

_____

_____

_____

_____

_____

_____

_____

_____

_____

LEAN ON JESUS

My help comes from the LORD, the Maker of heaven and earth. (Psalm 121:2)

You are God's child and, as a loving Father, He will watch over, protect, and help you. It doesn't always unfold the way we would like it to, but God never fails to make perfect decisions from an eternal perspective. Read Psalm 121 and journal what stands out to you.

_____

_____

_____

_____

_____

_____

_____

_____

_____

_____

_____

_____

_____

_____

INVEST IN PRAYER

In the same way, the Spirit helps us in our weakness. We do not know what we ought to pray for, but the Spirit himself intercedes for us through wordless groans. (Romans 8:26)

Thank Jesus for giving us the Holy Spirit, our Helper, and the power we have through Him. How often do you tap into this power? Journal your prayers.

_____

_____

_____

_____

_____

_____

_____

_____

_____

_____

_____

_____

_____

_____
_____
_____
_____
_____
_____

VALUE OTHERS

In everything I did, I showed you that by this kind of hard work we must help the weak, remembering the words the Lord Jesus himself said: It is more blessed to give than to receive. (Acts 20:35)

Do you know someone who struggles with depression or another form of mental illness? What can you do to support them in their time of need?

_____
_____
_____
_____
_____
_____

Action Plan

_____
_____
_____
_____
_____
_____

EMBRACE YOUR STORY

In your unfailing love you will lead the people you have redeemed.
Exodus 15:13)

List your top 3 go-to verses when facing challenges in life. If you have a story connected to any of those verses, write it down.

_____
_____
_____
_____
_____
_____
_____
_____
_____
_____
_____
_____
_____
_____
_____
_____
_____
_____
_____
_____

AFTER SOME TIME:

_____
_____
_____
_____
_____

6

Where Do You Stand?

Lukewarm Christianity doesn't work (see Revelation 3:15-16). In terms of your personal relationship with God through Jesus, there's no middle ground. Either you're in, or you're out. Maybe you are following a religion and think you must earn God's favor. There is no following Jesus AND...there's just Jesus.

DAY 1: GETTING OUT OF THE HEAT

DIGEST & REFRAME

For since the creation of the world God's invisible qualities-his eternal power and divine nature-have been clearly seen, being understood from what has been made, so that people are without excuse. (Romans 1:20)

Expand on the pause and reflect questions and any additional notes you made along the way.

What emotions did this section trigger and what did it stir inside you?

What is true in your story? What does Scripture say about your situation?

_____

_____

_____

_____

_____

_____

_____

_____

_____

_____

LEAN ON JESUS

Therefore God exalted him to the highest place and gave him the name that is above every name, that at the name of Jesus every knee should bow, in heaven and on earth and under the earth, and every tongue acknowledge that Jesus Christ is Lord, to the glory of God the Father. (Philippians 2:9-11)

In Mark 10:15, we are instructed to "receive the kingdom of God like a little child." We need this childlike, pure, faith in order to see our need for God and Jesus as our Savior. Lean into what this would look like for you.

_____

_____

_____

_____

_____

_____
_____
_____
_____
_____
_____
_____
_____
_____

INVEST IN PRAYER

Is anyone among you in trouble? Let them pray. Is anyone happy? Let them sing songs of praise. (James 5:13)

Write down your top 3 praise songs. Spend time this week singing songs of praise.

_____
_____
_____
_____
_____
_____
_____
_____
_____
_____
_____
_____
_____
_____
_____
_____

_____
_____
_____
_____
_____
_____

VALUE OTHERS

Dear children, let us not love with words or speech but with actions and in truth.
(1 John 3:18)

Send a note of appreciation to someone who has positively impacted your life through ministry.

_____
_____
_____
_____
_____
_____
_____
_____
_____

Action Plan

_____
_____
_____

EMBRACE YOUR STORY

In him we have redemption through his blood, the forgiveness of sins, in accordance with the riches of God's grace that he lavished on us.
(Ephesians 1:7-8)

What would you do if fear or insecurities were not holding you back?

_____

_____

_____

_____

_____

_____

_____

_____

_____

_____

_____

_____

_____

_____

_____

_____

_____

EXTRA NOTES:

_____

_____

_____

_____

DIGEST & REFRAME

For the word of God is alive and active. Sharper than any double-edged sword, it penetrates even to dividing soul and spirit, joints and marrow; it judges the thoughts and attitudes of the heart. (Hebrews 4:12)

Expand on the pause and reflect questions and any additional notes you made along the way.

What emotions did this section trigger and what did it stir inside you?

What is true in your story? What does Scripture say about your situation?

_____

_____

_____

_____

_____

_____

_____

_____

_____

_____

_____

LEAN ON JESUS

Therefore God exalted him to the highest place and gave him the name that is above every name, that at the name of Jesus every knee should bow, in heaven and on earth and under the earth, and every tongue acknowledge that Jesus Christ is Lord, to the glory of God the Father. (Philippians 2:9-11)

When was the last time God's word penetrated your soul? Could your heart need some softening?

_____

_____

_____

_____

INVEST IN PRAYER

Is anyone among you in trouble? Let them pray. Is anyone happy? Let them sing songs of praise. (James 5:13)

Pray for your church's children's ministry, especially those children that may pop in once in a while. Pray that the enemy doesn't snatch the word sown into them (Matthew 13:19). Journal your prayers.

DAY 2: PREPARE THE SOIL, cont.

_____

_____

_____

_____

_____

_____

VALUE OTHERS

Dear children, let us not love with words or speech but with actions and in truth.
(1 John 3:18)

Bless someone that is in children's ministry. Send them a card, treat, or a message of encouragement.

_____

_____

_____

_____

_____

_____

_____

_____

_____

Action Plan

_____

_____

_____

_____

_____

_____

EMBRACE YOUR STORY

In him we have redemption through his blood, the forgiveness of sins, in
accordance with the riches of God's grace that he lavished on us.
(Ephesians 1:7-8)

How is God transforming you from the inside out?

_____
_____
_____
_____
_____
_____
_____
_____
_____
_____
_____
_____
_____
_____
_____
_____
_____
_____

EXTRA NOTES:

_____
_____
_____
_____
_____

DIGEST & REFRAME

The secret of the kingdom of God has been given to you. (Mark 4:11)

Expand on the pause and reflect questions and any additional notes you made along the way.

What emotions did this section trigger and what did it stir inside you?

What is true in your story? What does Scripture say about your situation?

_____

_____

_____

_____

_____

_____

_____

_____

_____

_____

LEAN ON JESUS

Therefore God exalted him to the highest place and gave him the name that is above every name, that at the name of Jesus every knee should bow, in heaven and on earth and under the earth, and every tongue acknowledge that Jesus Christ is Lord, to the glory of God the Father. (Philippians 2:9-11)

Do you struggle between following man-made religious customs and having a personal relationship with God through Jesus? Seek the truth in the Scriptures and ask God to reveal this to you. Jesus calls out the Pharisees and the teachers of the law for their hypocrisy in Matthew 23. On the outside they appear religious, yet inside they are far from God. What about you—what's going on inside?

_____

_____

_____

_____
_____
_____
_____
_____
_____
_____
_____

INVEST IN PRAYER

Is anyone among you in trouble? Let them pray. Is anyone happy? Let them sing songs of praise. (James 5:13)

When sharing your faith, pray for the leading of the Holy Spirit and for wisdom, patience, and understanding. Journal your prayers.

_____
_____
_____
_____
_____
_____
_____
_____
_____
_____
_____
_____
_____
_____

_____
_____
_____
_____
_____
_____

VALUE OTHERS

Dear children, let us not love with words or speech but with actions and in truth.
(1 John 3:18)

If sharing Jesus with others is difficult for you, pray for boldness and for opportunities. As someone may have shared with you, do so for someone else. People need to hear the message of hope and redemption. People are hungry for the truth, and they are thirsty for living water (John 14:16 and John 7:37).

_____
_____
_____
_____
_____
_____

Action Plan

_____
_____
_____
_____
_____

DAY 3: PLANT THE SEED, cont.

EMBRACE YOUR STORY

In him we have redemption through his blood, the forgiveness of sins, in
accordance with the riches of God's grace that he lavished on us.
(Ephesians 1:7-8)

What do you believe God has called you to do?

_____

_____

_____

_____

_____

_____

_____

_____

_____

_____

_____

_____

_____

_____

_____

_____

_____

_____

EXTRA NOTES:

_____

_____

_____

_____

_____

DAY 4: THORNS AND THISTLES

DIGEST & REFRAME

Do not repay anyone evil for evil. Be careful to do what is right in the eyes of everyone. (Romans 12:18)

Expand on the pause and reflect questions and any additional notes you made along the way.

What emotions did this section trigger and what did it stir inside you?

What is true in your story? What does Scripture say about your situation?

_____

_____

_____

_____

_____

_____

_____

_____

_____

_____

LEAN ON JESUS

Therefore God exalted him to the highest place and gave him the name that is above every name, that at the name of Jesus every knee should bow, in heaven and on earth and under the earth, and every tongue acknowledge that Jesus Christ is Lord, to the glory of God the Father. (Philippians 2:9-11)

Do you carry any church-related wounds or unresolved trauma that are affecting your ability to fully trust in God's sovereignty?

_____

_____

_____

_____

_____

_____
_____
_____
_____
_____
_____
_____
_____
_____

INVEST IN PRAYER

Is anyone among you in trouble? Let them pray. Is anyone happy? Let them sing songs of praise. (James 5:13)

Pray for your enemies. Pray for those who persecute you for your faith. Journal your prayers.

_____
_____
_____
_____
_____
_____
_____
_____
_____
_____
_____
_____
_____
_____
_____
_____

DAY 4: THORNS AND THISTLES, cont.

_____

_____

_____

_____

_____

_____

VALUE OTHERS

Dear children, let us not love with words or speech but with actions and in truth.
(1 John 3:18)

What can you do to support your local prison ministry? Is there a family left behind that could use some care?

_____

_____

_____

_____

_____

_____

_____

Action Plan

_____

_____

_____

_____

_____

_____

_____

_____

EMBRACE YOUR STORY

In him we have redemption through his blood, the forgiveness of sins, in accordance with the riches of God's grace that he lavished on us.
(Ephesians 1:7-8)

Write about a mountain moving answer to prayer.

_____

_____

_____

_____

_____

_____

_____

_____

_____

_____

_____

_____

_____

_____

_____

_____

_____

_____

_____

EXTRA NOTES:

_____

_____

_____

_____

_____

DAY 5: THE MUSTARD SEED

DIGEST & REFRAME

And pray in the Spirit on all occasions with all kinds of prayers and requests.
With this in mind, be alert and always keep on praying for all the Lord's people.
(Ephesians 6:18)

Expand on the pause and reflect questions and any additional notes you made
along the way.

What emotions did this section trigger and what did it stir inside you?

What is true in your story? What does Scripture say about your situation?

LEAN ON JESUS

Therefore God exalted him to the highest place and gave him the name that is
above every name, that at the name of Jesus every knee should bow, in heaven
and on earth and under the earth, and every tongue acknowledge that Jesus
Christ is Lord, to the glory of God the Father. (Philippians 2:9-11)

Do you believe in the absolute truth that "at the name of Jesus every knee will
bow?"

_____
_____
_____
_____
_____
_____
_____
_____
_____

INVEST IN PRAYER

Is anyone among you in trouble? Let them pray. Is anyone happy? Let them sing songs of praise. (James 5:13)

Pray for the words to say when your faith gets questioned. Journal your prayers.

_____
_____
_____
_____
_____
_____
_____
_____
_____
_____
_____
_____
_____
_____

_____
_____
_____
_____
_____
_____

VALUE OTHERS

Dear children, let us not love with words or speech but with actions and in truth.
(1 John 3:18)

Listen to the Spirit's prompting and act on it when being moved to do something for someone. Pray for direction on what you can do to be the hands and feet of Jesus in your community.

_____
_____
_____
_____
_____
_____

Action Plan

EMBRACE YOUR STORY

In him we have redemption through his blood, the forgiveness of sins, in accordance with the riches of God's grace that he lavished on us.
(Ephesians 1:7-8)

Write out your testimony of faith, the day you surrendered your life to Jesus.

_____

_____

_____

_____

_____

_____

_____

_____

_____

_____

_____

_____

_____

_____

_____

_____

AFTER SOME TIME:

_____

_____

_____

_____

_____

7

How Will You Live?

We all love new things. Even if we purchase something used, it's new to us and this brings us joy, at least for a little while. Over time, the new becomes old, we lose interest in it, or something better comes along. This is not the case with the new life we have through Jesus. If you are seeking Him with a hunger to really know Him, this new life will never get old. The more I know Him, the greater my love is, and the more I want to sit in His presence.

DIGEST & REFRAME

Being confident of this, that he who began a good work in you will carry it on to completion until the day of Christ Jesus. (Philippians 1:6)

Expand on the pause and reflect questions and any additional notes you made along the way.

What emotions did this section trigger and what did it stir inside you?

What is true in your story? What does Scripture say about your situation?

_____

_____

_____

_____

_____

_____

_____

_____

_____

_____

_____

LEAN ON JESUS

Be strong and courageous. Do not be afraid or terrified because of them, for the LORD your God goes with you; he will never leave you nor forsake you. (Deuteronomy 31:6)

What does God ask of you? What is the promise of this verse?

_____

_____

_____

_____

_____

_____
_____
_____
_____
_____
_____
_____
_____
_____

INVEST IN PRAYER

And pray in the Spirit on all occasions with all kinds of prayers and requests.
(Ephesians 6:18)

We have permission to pray "all kinds of prayers." Everything, whether big or small, should be presented to God, because there is nothing beyond His reach.

_____
_____
_____
_____
_____
_____
_____
_____
_____
_____
_____
_____
_____
_____
_____
_____

_____
_____
_____
_____
_____
_____

VALUE OTHERS

Do nothing out of selfish ambition or vain conceit. Rather, in humility value others above yourselves, not looking to your own interests but each of you to the interests of the others. (Philippians 2:3-4)

Do something for someone without the expectation of receiving. Have groceries delivered for a family in need. Run an errand for a busy mother. Find a need and meet it. Don't ask for permission. Just bless them.

_____
_____
_____
_____
_____
_____
_____

Action Plan

_____
_____
_____
_____
_____
_____

EMBRACE YOUR STORY

Praise be to the Lord, the God of Israel, because he has come to his people and redeemed them. (Luke 1:68)

Write about a significant move in your life. This doesn't have to be a physical move from one location to the next. It could be a move from a job, relationship, or mindset.

_____

_____

_____

_____

_____

_____

_____

_____

_____

_____

_____

_____

_____

_____

_____

_____

_____

_____

EXTRA NOTES:

_____

_____

_____

_____

_____

DIGEST & REFRAME

I tell you, open your eyes and look at the fields! They are ripe for harvest.
(John 4:35)

Expand on the pause and reflect questions and any additional notes you made along the way.

What emotions did this section trigger and what did it stir inside you?

What is true in your story? What does Scripture say about your situation?

_____

_____

_____

_____

_____

_____

_____

_____

_____

LEAN ON JESUS

Be strong and courageous. Do not be afraid or terrified because of them, for the LORD your God goes with you; he will never leave you nor forsake you.
(Deuteronomy 31:6)

If you have lost sight of your faith, return to the love you had when you first came to Jesus. Ask God to put an unquenchable hunger for His word and continued intimacy with him. This is a relationship worth your effort and dedication.

_____

_____

_____

_____

_____

_____
_____
_____
_____
_____
_____
_____
_____
_____
_____

INVEST IN PRAYER

And pray in the Spirit on all occasions with all kinds of prayers and requests.
(Ephesians 6:18)

Pray for those people you have left in order to follow Christ.

_____
_____
_____
_____
_____
_____
_____
_____
_____
_____
_____
_____
_____
_____
_____
_____
_____

_____
_____
_____
_____
_____
_____

VALUE OTHERS

Do nothing out of selfish ambition or vain conceit. Rather, in humility value others above yourselves, not looking to your own interests but each of you to the interests of the others. (Philippians 2:3-4)

Does your church have a benevolence fund or committee to support its members in need? If so, how can you offer your support or possibly expand this ministry? If it doesn't, what steps can you take to make sure that no one is overlooked?

_____
_____
_____
_____
_____
_____

Action Plan

_____
_____
_____
_____
_____
_____

EMBRACE YOUR STORY

Praise be to the Lord, the God of Israel, because he has come to his people and redeemed them. (Luke 1:68)

What personal experiences have pulled you away or brought your closer to the church?

_____

_____

_____

_____

_____

_____

_____

_____

_____

_____

_____

_____

_____

_____

_____

_____

_____

_____

EXTRA NOTES:

_____

_____

_____

_____

_____

DIGEST & REFRAME

May the favor of the Lord our God rest on us; establish the work of our hands for us yes, establish the work of our hands. (Psalm 90:17)

Expand on the pause and reflect questions and any additional notes you made along the way.

What emotions did this section trigger and what did it stir inside you?

What is true in your story? What does Scripture say about your situation?

_____

_____

_____

_____

_____

_____

_____

_____

_____

_____

LEAN ON JESUS

Be strong and courageous. Do not be afraid or terrified because of them, for the LORD your God goes with you; he will never leave you nor forsake you. (Deuteronomy 31:6)

Has Jesus called you into something new? Lean on him for answers and directions for this chapter of your life.

_____

_____

_____

_____

_____

_____
_____
_____
_____
_____
_____
_____
_____
_____

INVEST IN PRAYER

And pray in the Spirit on all occasions with all kinds of prayers and requests.
(Ephesians 6:18)

What do you long to do as a profession? Ask God to help you recognize and seize the opportunities He presents. Don't let fear keep you from entering the plans God has for your life. Memorize Deuteronomy 31:6. Journal your prayers.

_____
_____
_____
_____
_____
_____
_____
_____
_____
_____
_____
_____
_____
_____
_____

_____

_____

_____

_____

_____

_____

VALUE OTHERS

Do nothing out of selfish ambition or vain conceit. Rather, in humility value others above yourselves, not looking to your own interests but each of you to the interests of the others. (Philippians 2:3-4)

Commit to going out of your way on Sunday mornings by welcoming a new person or introducing yourself to someone you may not have met.

_____

_____

_____

_____

_____

_____

_____

_____

Action Plan

_____

_____

_____

_____

_____

EMBRACE YOUR STORY

Praise be to the Lord, the God of Israel, because he has come to his people and redeemed them. (Luke 1:68)

What is your dream job? Have fun with this, even if it seems unrealistic. What does this say about your longings?

_____

_____

_____

_____

_____

_____

_____

_____

_____

_____

_____

_____

_____

_____

_____

_____

_____

_____

_____

EXTRA NOTES:

_____

_____

_____

_____

DIGEST & REFRAME

"For I know the plans I have for you," declares the LORD, "plans to prosper you and not to harm you, plans to give you hope and a future." (Jeremiah 29:11)

Expand on the pause and reflect questions and any additional notes you made along the way.

What emotions did this section trigger and what did it stir inside you?

What is true in your story? What does Scripture say about your situation?

_____

_____

_____

_____

_____

_____

_____

_____

_____

_____

_____

LEAN ON JESUS

Be strong and courageous. Do not be afraid or terrified because of them, for the LORD your God goes with you; he will never leave you nor forsake you.
(Deuteronomy 31:6)

Many of us are inclined to fear the unknown of what the future holds. How does leaning on Jesus help with overcoming this fear?

_____

_____

_____

_____

_____

_____
_____
_____
_____
_____
_____
_____
_____
_____

INVEST IN PRAYER

And pray in the Spirit on all occasions with all kinds of prayers and requests.
(Ephesians 6:18)

Think about a time of how God moved you in a direction you did not expect.
How did He meet your specific needs during this move? Journal your prayer of
gratitude.

_____
_____
_____
_____
_____
_____
_____
_____
_____
_____
_____
_____
_____

_____
_____
_____
_____
_____
_____

VALUE OTHERS

Do nothing out of selfish ambition or vain conceit. Rather, in humility value others above yourselves, not looking to your own interests but each of you to the interests of the others. (Philippians 2:3-4)

Do you know someone that needs to make a new move? How can you help them pack for this transition in life? What support from your resources can you offer? (financial, mentoring, something tangible)

_____
_____
_____
_____
_____
_____
_____

Action Plan

_____
_____
_____
_____
_____
_____

EMBRACE YOUR STORY

Praise be to the Lord, the God of Israel, because he has come to his people and redeemed them. (Luke 1:68)

What is your vision for the future? Who is there with you?

_____

_____

_____

_____

_____

_____

_____

_____

_____

_____

_____

_____

_____

_____

_____

_____

_____

EXTRA NOTES:

_____

_____

_____

_____

_____

DIGEST & REFRAME

I will give you a new heart and put a new spirit in you; I will remove from you your heart of stone and give you a heart of flesh. (Ezekiel 36:26)

Expand on the pause and reflect questions and any additional notes you made along the way.

What emotions did this section trigger and what did it stir inside you?

What is true in your story? What does Scripture say about your situation?

_____

_____

_____

_____

_____

_____

_____

_____

_____

_____

_____

LEAN ON JESUS

Be strong and courageous. Do not be afraid or terrified because of them, for the LORD your God goes with you; he will never leave you nor forsake you. (Deuteronomy 31:6)

What are you still holding on to from your old life that is keeping you from fully living a new life in Christ? Open your heart and allow Him to be the Lord over your life. Get to know Him through the Scriptures.

_____

_____

_____

_____

_____

INVEST IN PRAYER

And pray in the Spirit on all occasions with all kinds of prayers and requests.
(Ephesians 6:18)

Pray for the family of believers, the church. Pray that the church remains faithful to the Word without wavering. Journal your prayers.

_____
_____
_____
_____
_____
_____

VALUE OTHERS

Do nothing out of selfish ambition or vain conceit. Rather, in humility value others above yourselves, not looking to your own interests but each of you to the interests of the others. (Philippians 2:3-4)

Do you know of anyone who is currently dealing with an illness? Ask God how you can offer a helping hand in meeting some of their needs?

_____
_____
_____
_____
_____
_____
_____

Action Plan

_____
_____
_____
_____
_____
_____

EMBRACE YOUR STORY

Praise be to the Lord, the God of Israel, because he has come to his people and redeemed them. (Luke 1:68)

What is something new in your life that is bringing you great joy? Write about it, no matter what it is. We can enjoy new things in our life as long as we don't make them idols.

_____

_____

_____

_____

_____

_____

_____

_____

_____

_____

_____

_____

_____

_____

_____

_____

_____

AFTER SOME TIME:

_____

_____

_____

_____

_____

8

Ready To Surrender?

Surrender is not giving up, it's allowing God to take the lead. During tough times, it's not about bargaining with God or making empty promises; it's about trusting Him completely. It's having the faith to believe that He is in the unknown. Surrender means not wavering in the face of persecution because of Him. To fully surrender, we must deny ourselves, take up our cross and follow Him daily (Luke 9:23). It is the most difficult thing a human can do, yet nothing compares to the journey of allowing God to lead your steps.

DIGEST & REFRAME

Many are the plans in a person's heart, but it is the LORD's purpose that prevails. (Proverbs 19:21)

Expand on the pause and reflect questions and any additional notes you made along the way.

What emotions did this section trigger and what did it stir inside you?

What is true in your story? What does Scripture say about your situation?

_____

_____

_____

_____

_____

_____

_____

_____

_____

_____

LEAN ON JESUS

I pray that the eyes of your heart may be enlightened in order that you may know the hope to which he has called you, the riches of his glorious inheritance in his holy people, and his incomparably great power for us who believe. (Ephesians 1:18-19)

How do you react when life goes in a different direction or when your plans don't align with God's? What does leaning on Jesus look like during these times?

_____

_____

_____

_____

_____

_____

_____

_____

_____

_____

_____

_____

_____

INVEST IN PRAYER

Be still before the LORD and wait patiently for him. (Psalm 37:7)

Pray that God would reveal the things which you are holding too tightly. Journal your prayers.

_____

_____

_____

_____

_____

_____

_____

_____

_____

_____

_____

_____

_____

_____

_____

VALUE OTHERS

Whoever shuts their ears to the cry of the poor will also cry out and not be answered. (Proverbs 21:13)

What can you do to expand God's kingdom?

Action Plan

EMBRACE YOUR STORY

This is what the LORD says-your Redeemer, who formed you in the womb: I am the LORD, the Maker of all things. (Isaiah 44:24)

What is something you are good at? Give yourself permission to be proud of it.

_____

_____

_____

_____

_____

_____

_____

_____

_____

_____

_____

_____

_____

_____

_____

_____

EXTRA NOTES:

_____

_____

_____

_____

_____

DIGEST & REFRAME

But he said to me, "My grace is sufficient for you, for my power is made perfect in weakness." (2 Corinthians 12:9)

Expand on the pause and reflect questions and any additional notes you made along the way.

What emotions did this section trigger and what did it stir inside you?

What is true in your story? What does Scripture say about your situation?

_____

_____

_____

_____

_____

_____

_____

_____

_____

_____

LEAN ON JESUS

I pray that the eyes of your heart may be enlightened in order that you may know the hope to which he has called you, the riches of his glorious inheritance in his holy people, and his incomparably great power for us who believe. (Ephesians 1:18-19)

Are you struggling with a "thorn in the flesh," pleading with God to take it from you? (see 2 Corinthians 6-10) Write about this thorn. It doesn't have to be an illness, it can be a circumstance or even a person. What does it look like to lean on Jesus in this situation?

_____

_____

_____

_____

_____

_____

_____

_____

_____

_____

_____

_____

_____

_____

INVEST IN PRAYER

Be still before the LORD and wait patiently for him. (Psalm 37:7)

Pray for perseverance in trials and through the waiting. Journal your prayers.

_____

_____

_____

_____

_____

_____

_____

_____

_____

_____

_____

_____

_____

_____

_____

_____

_____

_____
_____
_____
_____
_____
_____

VALUE OTHERS

Whoever shuts their ears to the cry of the poor will also cry out and not be answered. (Proverbs 21:13)

Who around you is crying out for help? What do they need?

_____
_____
_____
_____
_____
_____
_____
_____

Action Plan

_____
_____
_____
_____
_____
_____

EMBRACE YOUR STORY

This is what the LORD says-your Redeemer, who formed you in the womb: I am the LORD, the Maker of all things. (Isaiah 44:24)

Running became my stress reliever, my drug of choice. What is something you run to as an escape? If it is consuming your time, thoughts and finances, could this possibly be an idol in your life? In everything we do, there must be a healthy balance. What determines this healthy balance for you?

_____

_____

_____

_____

_____

_____

_____

_____

_____

_____

_____

_____

_____

_____

_____

_____

_____

EXTRA NOTES:

_____

_____

_____

_____

_____

DIGEST & REFRAME

Ask and it will be given to you; seek and you will find; knock and the door will be opened to you. (Matthew 7:7)

Expand on the pause and reflect questions and any additional notes you made along the way.

What emotions did this section trigger and what did it stir inside you?

What is true in your story? What does Scripture say about your situation?

_____

_____

_____

_____

_____

_____

_____

_____

_____

_____

_____

_____

LEAN ON JESUS

I pray that the eyes of your heart may be enlightened in order that you may know the hope to which he has called you, the riches of his glorious inheritance in his holy people, and his incomparably great power for us who believe. (Ephesians 1:18-19)

Can you trust that God's grace is sufficient for you and his power is made perfect in your weakness? Ask God to give you supernatural faith to trust Him, even when circumstances make little sense.

_____

_____

_____

_____

_____

_____

_____

_____

_____

_____

_____

_____

_____

_____

INVEST IN PRAYER

Be still before the LORD and wait patiently for him. (Psalm 37:7)

The strength to overcome and persevere in any situation has already been given to us by God through the Holy Spirit. The same power that raised Jesus from the dead lives in us. We can overcome through the power of the Holy Spirit. Although this can be challenging, we must make an effort to get to know the source of this power in order to live by it. Seek to know the Holy Spirit's power in your life. Journal your prayers.

_____

_____

_____

_____

_____

_____

_____

_____

_____

_____

_____

_____

_____

_____
_____
_____
_____
_____
_____

VALUE OTHERS

Whoever shuts their ears to the cry of the poor will also cry out and not be answered. (Proverbs 21:13)

Listen with the heart of the Spirit, not only with your ears. We can learn a lot from the body language of someone speaking to us through their lack of eye contact, poor posture, or fidgeting. Look at the person speaking to you through the eyes of Jesus. How can you put this into practice and become more mindful of how you listen?

_____
_____
_____
_____
_____
_____

Action Plan

_____
_____
_____
_____
_____
_____

EMBRACE YOUR STORY

This is what the LORD says-your Redeemer, who formed you in the womb: I am the LORD, the Maker of all things. (Isaiah 44:24)

Which door are you longing to be opened in your life?

_____

_____

_____

_____

_____

_____

_____

_____

_____

_____

_____

_____

_____

_____

_____

_____

EXTRA NOTES:

_____

_____

_____

_____

DIGEST & REFRAME

He is not here; he has risen, just as he said. (Matthew 28:6)

Expand on the pause and reflect questions and any additional notes you made along the way.

What emotions did this section trigger and what did it stir inside you?

What is true in your story? What does Scripture say about your situation?

_____

_____

_____

_____

_____

_____

_____

_____

_____

_____

_____

LEAN ON JESUS

I pray that the eyes of your heart may be enlightened in order that you may know the hope to which he has called you, the riches of his glorious inheritance in his holy people, and his incomparably great power for us who believe.
(Ephesians 1:18-19)

What did the sketch, God's Child, provoke in you? Could you see yourself as a child in God's hands?

_____

_____

_____

_____

_____

_____
_____
_____
_____
_____
_____
_____
_____
_____

INVEST IN PRAYER

Be still before the LORD and wait patiently for him. (Psalm 37:7)

Have you experienced a pause in your plans and it turned out to be a redirection for a better path God had for you? Write about it along with a prayer of gratitude.

_____
_____
_____
_____
_____
_____
_____
_____
_____
_____
_____
_____
_____
_____
_____

_____
_____
_____
_____
_____
_____

VALUE OTHERS

Whoever shuts their ears to the cry of the poor will also cry out and not be answered. (Proverbs 21:13)

Who is in desperate need of a miracle right now? How can you best support this person?

_____
_____
_____
_____
_____
_____
_____
_____

Action Plan

_____
_____
_____
_____
_____

EMBRACE YOUR STORY

This is what the LORD says-your Redeemer, who formed you in the womb: I am
the LORD, the Maker of all things. (Isaiah 44:24)

Write a letter to your future self, describing a goal you aim to accomplish in
the coming year. Then write the first thing you are going to do to get started
on this goal.

_____
_____
_____
_____
_____
_____
_____
_____
_____
_____
_____
_____
_____
_____
_____
_____
_____

EXTRA NOTES:

_____
_____
_____
_____
_____

DIGEST & REFRAME

Now to him who is able to do immeasurably more than all we ask or imagine, according to his power that is at work within us, to him be glory in the church and in Christ Jesus throughout all generations, for ever and ever! Amen.
(Ephesians 3:20-21)

Expand on the pause and reflect questions and any additional notes you made along the way.

What emotions did this section trigger and what did it stir inside you?

What is true in your story? What does Scripture say about your situation?

_____

_____

_____

_____

_____

_____

_____

_____

_____

_____

LEAN ON JESUS

I pray that the eyes of your heart may be enlightened in order that you may know the hope to which he has called you, the riches of his glorious inheritance in his holy people, and his incomparably great power for us who believe.
(Ephesians 1:18-19)

When was the last time you received a personal message from God? Was it through a friend, sermon, scripture, or song? What was the message?

_____

_____

_____

_____

_____

_____
_____
_____
_____
_____
_____
_____
_____
_____

INVEST IN PRAYER

Be still before the LORD and wait patiently for him. (Psalm 37:7)

If you haven't heard God speak to you recently, take a moment to sit in silence, read your favorite Psalm, or listen to praise music. Drop your defenses and welcome the Holy Spirit's presence to move in you. Journal your experience.

_____
_____
_____
_____
_____
_____
_____
_____
_____
_____
_____
_____
_____
_____

_____
_____
_____
_____
_____
_____

VALUE OTHERS

Whoever shuts their ears to the cry of the poor will also cry out and not be answered. (Proverbs 21:13)

Do you know of someone that could benefit from a retreat? What steps can your group of friends take to make this happen?

_____
_____
_____
_____
_____
_____
_____

Action Plan

_____
_____
_____
_____
_____
_____

EMBRACE YOUR STORY

This is what the LORD says-your Redeemer, who formed you in the womb: I am the LORD, the Maker of all things. (Isaiah 44:24)

Write about your ideal retreat. Go all out as if money were not an option.

_____

_____

_____

_____

_____

_____

_____

_____

_____

_____

_____

_____

_____

_____

_____

_____

_____

_____

_____

_____

_____

AFTER SOME TIME:

_____

_____

_____

_____

_____

Journaling

WHEN MY CHILDREN WERE young, I gave them each a notebook and told them to write or draw what they were feeling and anything they wanted to express. As a child, I valued the impact journaling had on my life and wanted to equip my children with the same skills.

In our innate need to be heard, my children shared their notebook with me. They would write, often sharing their feelings or struggles, and place their notebook under my pillow. I acknowledged their words, gave them writing prompts and placed their notebook under their pillow. We agreed that whatever they wrote didn't have to be discussed openly unless they wanted to. This gave them permission to communicate freely. Through journaling they developed the practice of dumping their thoughts and feelings on paper.

Journaling gives us an uncensored voice on paper.

I realize journaling may not come easily to everyone. If this is you, begin by removing any preconceived ideas of what you think journaling should look like. The expressive writing I am describing is raw and unedited, not poetic or written in calligraphy. It is the kind of writing that welcomes your tears. The kind that will unleash emotions that may cause you to rip the page into shreds, and it will feel so good. Does this spark something in you? I hope so!

As you journal, allow yourself the freedom to release everything, creating a clearing for your soul. Expressive writing doesn't always have to be negative. I would encourage you to finish your daily writing on a positive note. Consider this as planting flower seeds in a barren field. Even if it's just one positive word. Plant it—write what you are grateful for. Write out your dreams. Write prayers of all kinds, answers to those prayers as they come and watch your garden grow!

Journaling Tips

- As you journal, don't correct your writing–no commas, periods, or proper grammar. You are not writing for a teacher.

- Find words for what you are feeling. Allow your emotions to flow freely instead of stifling or criticizing them. You can refer to the feelings wheel at the end of this section. This wheel may help you find a word that better describes what are experiencing.

- Write verses you wish to memorize, your prayers, and praises. Take notes on your insights from Scripture readings and what God is revealing to you.

- Don't worry about making sense out of what you write or keeping it organized. This will stop the flow. Just write.

- You can explore what you penned, or let it simmer. From my experience, dumping on paper causes negative thoughts to lose their power, and that is all it takes. I rarely go back to read these. Then, there are other times where it is important to dig deeper and explore. Allow room for this.

- If you want to keep something from being read, simply tear out the page and have a ceremonial burning. Write it down, then watch it burn. You already did the hard work of getting it out. You have brought the situation to light, which will make it easier to revisit, if needed.

- Don't write in codes. This will disconnect you emotionally and not allow you to purge appropriately.

- Writing is better than typing. If you can, write it out. This engages different parts of your brain that may help in retrieving memories. Likewise, it will connect you to your emotions, which will enable healthy processing and healing.

If your dream is to write your story, use these notes as a reference. Don't use this journal guide as a rough draft. This could distract you from complete vulnerability because you may censor your writing to avoid sharing personal details in your book. This will hold you back from purging all of your thoughts and emotions.

My prayer for you is that journaling becomes a tool for healing and spiritual growth that you can use throughout your life.

Commit to completing this journey. Don't quit on yourself.

FEELINGS WHEEL

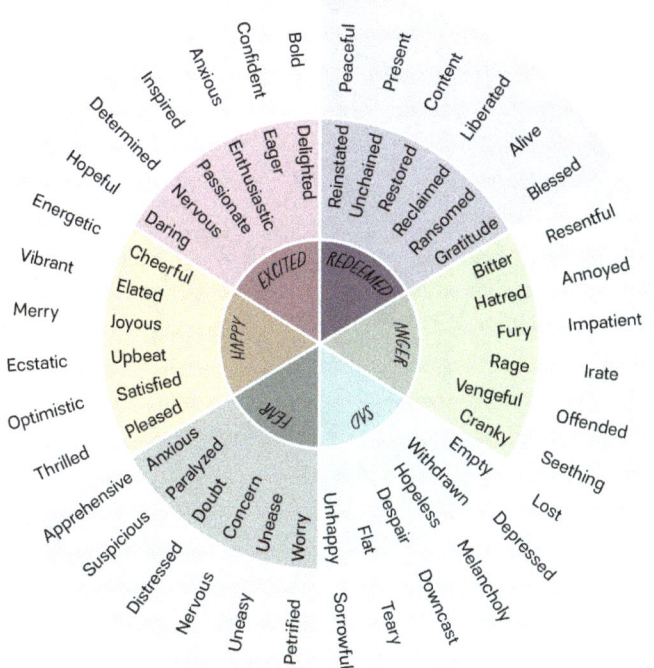

About The Author

Solé Wright is a Certified Fitness Trainer and Lifestyle Wellness Coach who guides women in overcoming personal challenges. She understands the impact of unresolved trauma on personal and spiritual growth. Her approach to health and wellness is to care for the whole person—body, mind, and soul.

After raising four children, she is pursuing her dream of sharing her redemptive story and how Jesus has met her on this journey. She enjoys a strong cup of coffee, reading, hiking and taking long walks. Solé and her husband live in Traverse City, Michigan, where they dote over their grandchildren.

She wants to hear from her readers you can message her at sole@solewright.com.

The companion book to *Time to Live*

For more information go to
https://www.solewright.com/